# INDIGENOUS HISTORY FROM 1865–1890
# THE POST–CIVIL WAR ERA

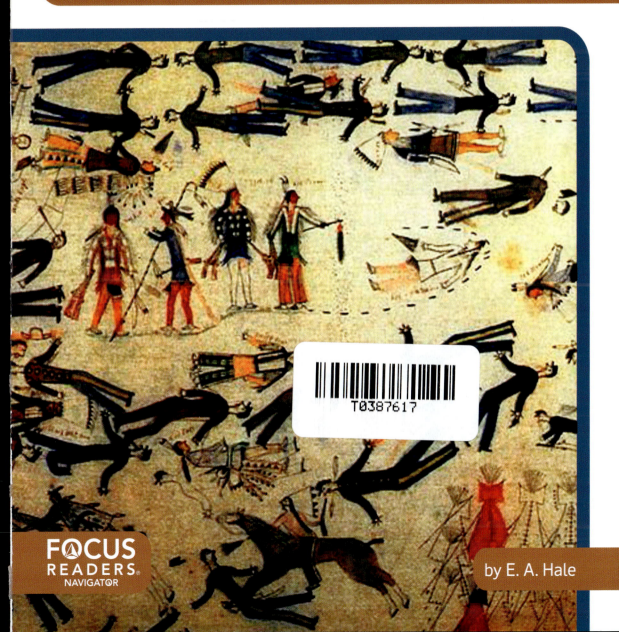

by E. A. Hale

WWW.FOCUSREADERS.COM

Copyright © 2025 by Focus Readers®, Mendota Heights, MN 55120. All rights reserved. No part of this book may be reproduced or utilized in any form or by any means without written permission from the publisher.

Focus Readers is distributed by North Star Editions:
sales@northstareditions.com | 888-417-0195

Produced for Focus Readers by Red Line Editorial.

Content Consultant: Katrina Phillips, PhD, Red Cliff Band of Lake Superior Ojibwe, Associate Professor of History, Macalester College

Photographs ©: History and Art Collection/Alamy, cover, 1, 26; National Archives, 4–5; Library of Congress, 6, 20, 24–25; John Dare Howland/Library of Congress, 9; Norval H. Busey/IanDagnall Computing/Alamy, 10–11; D. F. Barry/Library of Congress, 13; Pictorial Press Ltd/Alamy, 15; Quinton Smith/USFWS, 17; Pollock & Boyden/Graphic House/Archive Photos/Getty Images, 18–19; Red Line Editorial, 23; Corbis Historical/Getty Images, 29

**Library of Congress Cataloging-in-Publication Data**
Library of Congress Cataloging-in-Publication Data is available on the Library of Congress website.

**ISBN**
979-8-88998-411-5 (hardcover)
979-8-88998-439-9 (paperback)
979-8-88998-491-7 (ebook pdf)
979-8-88998-467-2 (hosted ebook)

Printed in the United States of America
Mankato, MN
012025

## ABOUT THE TERMINOLOGY
The terms **American Indians** and **Native Americans** are used interchangeably throughout this book. With more than 570 federally recognized tribes or nations in the United States, the usage will vary. Native nations and their people may use either term. The term **Indigenous peoples** describes groups of people who have lived in an area since prehistory. It may also be used as a shorter term to describe the federal designation **American Indians, Alaska Natives, and Native Hawaiians**.

## ABOUT THE AUTHOR
E. A. Hale is a proud member of the Choctaw Nation of Oklahoma.

# TABLE OF CONTENTS

**CHAPTER 1**
## Indigenous Lands 5

**CHAPTER 2**
## Tug of War 11

**VOICES FROM THE PAST**
## The Buffalo Go 16

**CHAPTER 3**
## Forced Removals 19

**CHAPTER 4**
## Reservation Life 25

Focus Questions • 30
Glossary • 31
To Learn More • 32
Index • 32

**CHAPTER 1**

# INDIGENOUS LANDS

The US Civil War ended in 1865. The United States was no longer at war with itself. As a result, it continued expanding west. US **settlers** moved across the Great Plains on trains and wagons. There were wide-open spaces. Farmlands were rich. Miners found gold. Many families moved from crowded cities.

Ely Parker of the Seneca Nation was one of many Native people in the Civil War. Parker wrote the surrender terms of the South.

Red Cloud was a respected Oglala Lakota leader from 1865 until his death in 1909.

There was one big problem. Hundreds of **Indigenous** groups already lived in the West. It was part of **Indian Country**. Many Native nations had lived there for thousands of years. And all had their own languages and **cultures**. Even so, settlers claimed land in Indian Country.

The United States often took Indigenous lands through wars or **treaties**. Congress made approximately 370 treaties with Native nations. The

## THE NAVAJO TREATY OF 1868

In 1868, the Diné, or Navajo, Nation lived on a **reservation**. It was in present-day New Mexico. The United States had forced them to leave their homelands in 1864. Their homelands were where Utah, Colorado, Arizona, and New Mexico meet. Soldiers had marched Diné people hundreds of miles. This journey was called the Navajo Long Walk. The Diné women banded together to negotiate. Then the Navajo Nation and the United States signed a peace treaty in 1868. Diné people returned to their homelands.

treaties started in 1778. These were legal agreements. Some treaties promised money, peace, and new places to live. The United States promised to take care of American Indians. But the tribes would have to move.

Native nations were not happy with the treaties. They did not want to give up their homes and lands. They did not trust the United States. Tribes learned treaties did not last. US leaders threatened to keep treaty money. They also warned tribes. Native nations *must* sign treaties. Otherwise, there would be no peace. The US Army would invade tribal lands. A war could destroy a tribe.

In 1867, the United States signed the Medicine Lodge Treaty with the Kiowa, Comanche, Arapaho, Cheyenne, and Plains Apache nations.

Then, in 1871, the United States stopped making treaties with Native nations. Congress passed the Indian Appropriations Act. No tribes were asked to help write it. The act said tribes were no longer **sovereign** nations. Instead, Congress passed laws about Native nations.

CHAPTER 2

# TUG OF WAR

By 1871, most Native nations had been moved to smaller areas. The US Army was too strong. Native nations wanted to protect their people. So, most had signed treaties. But some battles raged. They were about land rights. Fierce warriors fought soldiers. Battles also happened when the United States broke treaties.

Sarah Winnemucca was a Northern Paiute leader. She worked to force the United States to improve reservation conditions.

For example, bands of the Sioux Nation signed a peace treaty with the United States in April 1868. The treaty promised the Black Hills to the Lakota Sioux. These lands were included in the Great Sioux Reservation. But in 1874, miners illegally found gold on these lands. So, the United States wanted to buy the lands. The tribe refused to sell.

In response, the United States gave the Lakota an order. It told them all to go to the reservation. But the Lakota did not go. So, US troops took action. They tried to force the Lakota groups to go.

The Battle of Little Bighorn was in 1876. Many Lakota warriors rallied. They

Lakota leader Sitting Bull responded to the US offer to buy the Black Hills. He picked up a pinch of dirt. He said he wouldn't even sell that pinch of dirt.

had to defend their land. They had to protect their people. US soldiers tried to surprise attack the tribe. But the soldiers did not know there were so many warriors. The warriors won.

The Red River War was fought from 1874 to 1875 in West Texas. It traced back to the Medicine Lodge Treaty of

1867. The treaty promised food, hunting grounds, and reservations. Native people were sent to reservations. Some did not stay there. The US government broke its promises. It sent too little food. Settlers moved into reservations. Buffalo hunters camped on sacred hunting grounds.

## BISON HUNTS

From 1871 to 1884, buffalo hunters killed millions of bison. *Bison* is the scientific term for "buffalo." Hunters killed for sport. Bison were an important food source for Indigenous peoples. General Philip Sheridan said the United States must get rid of the bison. He said doing so would get rid of Native people. Without this important food source, the wars would end.

Settlers stand by thousands of bison skulls in 1892.

In response, Native warriors raided the camp. Settlers demanded the raids stop. These things led to more conflicts. Then the US Army declared war. It pressured the tribes until they surrendered.

# VOICES FROM THE PAST

# THE BUFFALO GO

A Kiowa woman named Old Lady Horse told a folktale. Her story told how the Kiowa Tribe had always hunted buffalo. They used the animals for food, clothing, and shelter. The buffalo were even part of their religion. The land, the buffalo, and Indigenous people were connected.

After the buffalo hunters came, only a few hundred buffalo were left. All the others had died in the mass killings on the plains. The buffalo knew their time was over. So the great herd met. They chose to leave.

Early one morning, a young woman looked across a creek. The mist was heavy. She had a vision. She watched a spirit buffalo herd appear. The buffalo walked to the mountain. The mountain face opened up.

Inside the mountain was lush green grass for the buffalo. The rivers were clear. The trees

The mountain in Old Lady Horse's folktale is part of the Wichita Mountains in Oklahoma.

bloomed inside the mountain slopes. It was beautiful. The last herd walked into the opening. They were never seen again.

**CHAPTER 3**

# FORCED REMOVALS

The Lakota victory after Little Bighorn did not last. Congress passed an act in 1877. It took the Black Hills from the Lakota. It did not honor the 1868 treaty.

Indigenous peoples did not want to change their ways of life. Some tribes hid in forests or swamps. Some roamed in unsettled lands. Others fought for their

> Beginning in the 1870s, thousands of settlers came to the Black Hills to mine gold. Mining harmed the environment there.

Chief Ouray (left) and Chipeta (right) were leaders of the Ute nation. They worked hard for peace and to prevent forced relocation.

homelands. They wanted to keep their ways of life. But they could not. Many tribes used peaceful ways. They spoke to Congress about past treaties. The US government made them move anyway.

Many tribes were forced to move more than once. Families carried belongings for miles. There was not enough to eat.

In 1881, soldiers force-marched the Ute tribe from Colorado to Utah. They ended up in a place they had never lived.

## THE TRAIL OF TEARS

Five tribes were forced to move along the Trail of Tears. The tribes were Choctaw Nation, Seminole Nation, Muscogee (Creek) Nation, Chickasaw Nation, and Cherokee Nation. Soldiers removed nearly 100,000 Native people from southeastern states to **Indian Territory**. The US government began these forced removals in the 1830s. They were based on unfair treaties. The removals are sometimes called the Cherokee Trail of Tears. That's because 4,000 Cherokee people died on the 1,000-mile (1,610-km) trek. People lacked food and warm clothing. They got sick.

The last big battle happened in 1886. It took place near an Arizona reservation. Apache warriors had fought against forced relocation. They fought for food. Geronimo, an Apache leader, finally handed his gun to a US general. The lives of his people were at stake. His men promised to quit fighting.

The United States changed course after the fighting ended. Congress passed the Dawes Act in 1887. The Dawes Act had many parts. It sold tribal lands to settlers. It broke up reservation lands. It gave **allotments** to Native families. The act promised that American Indians could be US citizens. It said their children must go to US schools. The Dawes Act tried to do away with tribal governments. This did not happen. But the act greatly harmed Native nations. They lost tens of millions of acres of land in the years to come.

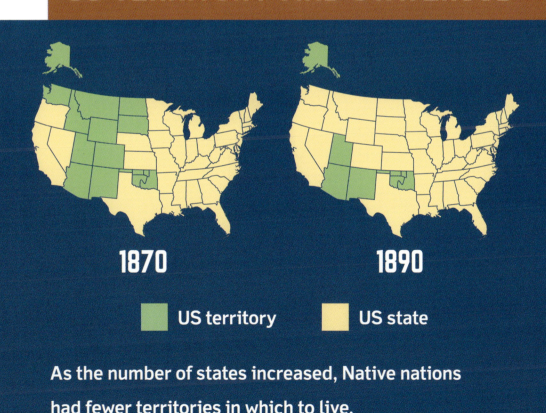

## US TERRITORY AND STATEHOOD

1870    1890

■ US territory    ■ US state

As the number of states increased, Native nations had fewer territories in which to live.

**CHAPTER 4**

# RESERVATION LIFE

Life was tough when Native people arrived on reservations. Some lands were wilderness. Other lands had too little rainfall. It was hard to find or grow food. Conditions were crowded. The US government offered to build schools and meeting houses. But these took time to build. In the meantime, people

Reservations tried to force Indigenous people to depend on the US government for basic needs.

25

Susan La Flesche saw white doctors provide poor care on the Omaha Reservation. In response, she became the first Native person to receive a US medical degree.

needed shelter. They made homes from natural resources. In the winter, families stayed close for warmth. They owned too few blankets. There were not enough warm clothes. Animal skins and furs were scarce.

The United States offered farm equipment. But Native people had hunted or gathered food before. They wanted to keep their ways of life. The US government also promised food and

## NATIVE SOVEREIGNTY

The US Constitution recognizes the rights of Indigenous peoples in multiple ways. One is Native sovereignty. Native nations have the right to create their own laws. They decide on tribal education, health care, and culture. Native nations decide how to care for their citizens or tribal members. The United States took away some Native rights. It took part of their power and land. But taking away some tribal rights does not erase Native sovereignty.

supplies. But they gave people too little. Some people starved. Children died. Still, Native people found ways to survive. They planted crops. They raised farm animals.

Congress continued to force Native nations to change. It made new acts and laws. It kept tight control on tribes. These actions chipped away at Native cultures. But Indigenous peoples survived. They kept their cultures alive. They practiced traditions. Nations wrote down their languages. They kept tribal sovereignty.

For example, some Indigenous peoples practiced the Ghost Dance. They hoped it would help them survive. US leaders banned the Ghost Dance. But tribes

The Ghost Dance spread throughout the United States in the late 1800s. Many Native nations took part.

practiced it anyway. In 1890, US soldiers punished the Sioux for the dance. Soldiers killed hundreds of men, women, and children. The deaths were near Wounded Knee Creek in South Dakota. Some called this the Wounded Knee Massacre. Even so, Native people continued resisting. They kept practicing their ways of life.

# FOCUS QUESTIONS

*Write your answers on a separate piece of paper.*

1. Write a paragraph explaining the main ideas of Chapter 4.

2. Do you think the tribes should have fought battles to keep their homelands? Why or why not?

3. Which Native nation was part of the Battle of Little Bighorn?
    - **A.** Navajo
    - **B.** Lakota
    - **C.** Kiowa

4. Which group was most harmed by forced removals?
    - **A.** Congress
    - **B.** Native nations
    - **C.** US settlers

*Answer key on page 32.*

# GLOSSARY

**allotments**
Land given to Native people for farming and ranching.

**cultures**
The customs, arts, beliefs, and laws of groups of people.

**Indian Country**
Native places and spaces in the United States, including reservations. It is home to hundreds of Native nations.

**Indian Territory**
Land reserved for forced relocation of many Native nations. The land later became eastern Oklahoma.

**Indigenous**
Native to a region, or belonging to ancestors who lived in a region before colonists arrived.

**reservation**
Land set aside by the US government for a Native nation.

**settlers**
People who move into an area and take control.

**sovereign**
Having the power to make rules and decisions without being controlled by another country.

**treaties**
Official agreements made between countries or groups.

# TO LEARN MORE

## BOOKS
Bird, F. A. *Navajo*. Minneapolis: Abdo Publishing, 2022.
Loh-Hagan, Virginia. *Indigenous Rights*. Ann Arbor, MI: Cherry Lake Publishing, 2022.
Sorell, Traci. *We Are Still Here! Native American Truths Everyone Should Know*. Watertown, MA: Charlesbridge Publishing, 2021.

## NOTE TO EDUCATORS
Visit **www.focusreaders.com** to find lesson plans, activities, links, and other resources related to this title.

# INDEX

Apache people, 22

Battle of Little Bighorn, 12–13, 19
Black Hills, 12, 19

Cherokee Nation, 21
Chickasaw Nation, 21
Choctaw Nation, 21

Dawes Act, 22–23

Geronimo, 22
Ghost Dance, 28–29

Indian Appropriations Act, 9

Kiowa Tribe, 16

Medicine Lodge Treaty, 13–14
Muscogee (Creek) Nation, 21

Navajo Long Walk, 7
Navajo Nation, 7

Old Lady Horse, 16

Red River War, 13–15

Seminole Nation, 21
Sioux Nation, 12, 29

Trail of Tears, 21

Ute tribe, 21

Wounded Knee Massacre, 29

Answer Key: 1. Answers will vary. 2. Answers will vary. 3. B. 4. B